AN L.A. GIRL'S GUIDE TO MANIFESTING

Manifesting Tools For Everyone

WRITTEN BY:
DAWN MICHELLE HOFFMAN

TABLE OF CONTENTS

Manifestation is when your dreams are pulled down from heaven and set before you on Earth.

At the end of every rainbow is a pot of gold and inside are your dreams waiting to come true…

Manifestation is Magic! Become the Magician in your life.

Dedication

I dedicate this book to my Teachers.
I am thankful for the life lessons
I have experienced.
They have helped me look beyond what was being made available. They have helped me remember the truth of the
universe when I have forgotten.
I am thankful for every step of this journey.
I learned to think outside the box.
I am thankful that the box has now disappeared.

INTRODUCTION TO MANIFESTATION

What is Manifestation?

Manifestation is:

a. One of the forms in which someone or something, such as a person, a divine being or an idea is revealed.

b. An act of creation from your mind. We are creating good or bad according to our thoughts.

It's amazing once I started intentionally co-creating in my life what miracles started to unfold. I saw that I have been manifesting all my life and just didn't realize it.

In New Age teachings, New Thought, law of attraction and The Secret we are taught that what we put our focus on will manifest in our lives. Whether it is positive or negative. I believe this is mostly true. I do not believe and have not seen the evidence that if I keep thinking that my sports team (The Lakers) will win that they will every time. Or if I keep hoping to be the President of the United States, at this point in my life, it's going to happen. I have had a few cases where I wished for things and was not specific and those things showed up in ways I certainly did not expect. We will get to those a little later.

I have been practicing a Manifestation technique with my friend Michelle for about 15 years. We were and still are exploring difference rituals, spiritual practices, philosophies and paths to personal growth and deeper compassion for others. Through our personal practice combining pieces of different modalities and teachings, we have been able to manifest, bring clarity and what we needed into our lives.

I started sharing this practice with others 6 years ago. I have had much success and many stories of people co-creating with God, the Universe, Source or whatever you may call it. When we understand that life doesn't have to just happen to us we are more at peace. That we can ask and be very specific about what we want and we will most certainly receive at the level we feel we deserve. What I mean by this is that sometimes we ask for things we are not quite ready to receive. We are so full of hope and yet we haven't cleared the path to be ready to fully receive that which we are asking for. Therefore it is important to start the process by looking at yourself, your old habits or patterns blocking you from fully receiving.

When I look back at the intentions I have set over the years, I see what I thought I was ready for and/or was asking for were not what I really needed. This is not to negate any part of the manifesting process. I've learned overtime that I may not have been asking for the right reasons. Intention is just as important as the things you are trying to manifest.

I also believe that being in touch with your intuition is a big part of successful manifesting. We all have an entire blueprint inside of us for our own lives. We know what is good for us and what is not. Often we ignore our "gut feelings" to be and have what our families, friends or the world is telling us we should. We should get to know ourselves, what our wants and needs truly are to bring us happiness.

Once we get in the flow and start practicing, we will start to attract, see evidence and manifest who and what is for the highest and best in our lives for our growth.

We will become MASTER MANIFESTORS!

Quotes on Manifesting

There are many quotes, philosophies and scriptures that confirm the importance of setting clear intentions to bring in to our lives what we desire.

Write it plain on tablets so that a herald can take it to God and though it may tarry…wait for it. When it manifests you will not remember the waiting. – Habakkuk 2:2-3

When seeking something material begin by knowing that you are an abundant being living in a universe that supports you in having everything you need to be happy. – Unknown

The Universe knows how to arrange the means for all my blessings. – Alan Cohen

The Power of Conscious Choice is your profit earning capital. Pay Attention!!! Watch over that moment of power! – Rumi

Knock and it will be opened. Seek and you shall find. Ask and it shall be given. For everyone who asks is given. everyone who seeks shall find. For everyone who knocks, doors open. – Luke 11:9:10

Be the Change you wish to see in the World – Gandhi

You are a child of God. Your playing small does not serve the World. There is nothing enlightened about shrinking down, so that others won't feel insecure around you. We were born to manifest the glory of God within us.
– Marianne Williamson

3 Types of Manifesting

There are many ways to Manifest what we seek in our lives.
I am going to focus on 3 Types of Manifestation I have seen
in action. In this chapter, I will share some examples of manifesting
without really trying, as well as manifesting
with non-specific and specific intent.

Some of my early Manifestations happened without me
even knowing what I was really asking for. They showed
up in ways I hadn't imagined. I would say that this place
of truly letting go of any attachment has turned out to be the key to
my increased trust in God, The Universe, Source and taking care of
all my needs. I say needs, because there are many things that I
have wanted over the years, I pleaded and begged for in a not so
graceful way, that I definitely did not "need". In retrospect not
getting those things have turned into blessings for me.

Manifesting Without Awareness

This is manifesting from your thoughts without intending to.

When I first moved to Los Angeles, I would drive down Sunset Blvd and see billboards with Angelyne on them (Google her if you do not know who she is). I'd laugh and say, "I want to be on a Billboard! If she can be seen by the world, than I certainly can." I just saw a platinum blonde in a pink Corvette and had no idea who she was and why she was up there. I just wanted to have a billboard like her. I would think of it every time I'd pass it. Shortly after, I started working for a Caribbean Art Gallery called Galerie Lakaye. The owners had also created The Earth Henna Tattoo Kit. They were creating the cover for the kit and asked me to be the hand model. My "Billboard" has been my hand all over the World for the past 17 years.

I wasn't seriously setting this intention and therefore had no idea it would show up much less how it did.

Another example of manifesting happened after my Dad moved to a small town in Oklahoma. Houses were really inexpensive. Houses that would sell for $1million in Los Angeles were being sold for less than $50,000. I joked about buying one and he asked me why. I heard that in the history of the town of less than 100 people there had never been a black family living there. I joked: and said that I was going to integrate the town. A few months later, a house came up for sale. My Stepmother had known the family her whole life. I asked to if she would find out the "locals price. They sold it to me for ½ the asking. I was lucky enough to rent it for several years to lovely, happy renters. My last renter was the first black man to live in the town. I was in the process of selling the house to him but the sale fell through. He got transferred to a position in a bigger city a few hours away. My manifestation came to fruition through the rental but fell short of being able to manifest the sale.

Manifesting with Non-Specific Intent

This type of manifesting is saying what you'd like but not being clear. Manifesting without being specific can get interesting. I have had what I have "sort of" asked for show up and was conflicted by what to do. I mean, I asked for it.

One example is that I was ready to meet someone with whom I could see myself wanting to build a long-term relationship. I had been divorced for quite sometime and a little commitment phobic. I wrote: "I'd like to attract a marriage minded man" on my list and let it go. A few months later, I met someone through a work friendship. He was marriage minded but definitely for a green card and not for love. If I ever put that on my list again, I will be sure to be specific as to the details like marriage minded in the same way as me. He is someone who is looking for healthy, lasting, supportive and uplifting love.

One year I wrote: "I am a published author" on my list, Again, not very specific. I was asked to submit one of my manifestation stories to be a part of a book on Manifesting. The request came from a workshop participant. Awesome I manifested what I asked for!!! I am a "published author"!!! I am published and yet I can't really claim it. The author chose not to credit anyone who shared their stories. I needed to add, "I am a credited, published author".

California and an Ocean View.

Several years ago my Mom and Sister moved from California to Buffalo, NY. Brrrrrrrr! I know!! Understandably, there was a large amount of complaining about the cold and a large desire to get back to California. In all my infinite manifesting wisdom, I advised my Mom to start being grateful for where she is and from that place of Gratitude, ask for what she would like to manifest.
A few months later, I was on a job in Cleveland, Ohio and had decided to surprise my Family and drive to Buffalo before heading back home. As I was driving I called my Mom, She thought I was waiting on my flight home to Los Angeles. She told me that she had been practicing what I suggested. She had been focusing on California and an Ocean view.
I will leave out the details of the Shock and Excitement that followed upon my arrival. I asked my Mom to be ready to leave at 10a the next day. As part of the surprise, I had set up an appointment with a realtor to look for houses for her. She was running low on funds and renting wasn't the best option for her. We looked at 12 houses that next day and the only one that was move in ready was on California Street. When we walked inside there was a mural of the ocean on the wall. Of course I asked her if this was the home for her or if perhaps she wasn't specific enough. I ended up buying that house for her. She still hopes to move back to California so this one was a steppingstone.

RealtyUSA

Manifesting with Specific Intent

This type of manifesting is being clear in your vision. Feeling what it will feel like when you have it and holding the energy of it.

Houses @ The Beach

Somehow this girl who spent most of her life within a few miles of the beach, ended up in The Valley. When my lease came up I decided to get myself back near the water. I wanted to find a place that had a little yard, no shared walls, parking and most importantly, an easy bike ride and/or walk to the beach. I headed to Venice Beach and looked at a few small apartments that were not a match. I headed home and looked online again. I saw an ad for a bungalow that seemed like exactly what I asked for. I made an appointment with Mr. White and headed back to Venice. I filled out the application and gave a deposit immediately. I was super excited. I was moving to Venice!! Later that night, I got a call from Mrs. White. She was calling to tell me her husband made a terrible mistake. She said for the past 25 years, he had never rented the property and she would have to meet me before allowing me to rent. Thankfully, I made a good impression and I moved in just a few weeks later!

The thing about manifesting is that we often get even better than we expected. After almost a year of living in the bungalow, a friend who lived around the corner was moving to Australia. He offered me his place that had a yard, was 4 times the size of mine, had parking, an office space, a beautiful lemon tree, an additional bedroom, was only a few hundred dollars more a month and it was 5 houses away. I was happy at the "LEMON TREE" house for several years. My good was expanding.

After a few years at the Lemon tree house, I was informed, that the house was being sold. I gave myself permission to pout for a full 24 hours. I told anyone who cared and some who didn't about this terrible news. The next day, I sat feeling clear of all my resistance to this change was out of my control and going to happen if I wanted it to or not. I prayed, "Thank you for the wonderful opportunity to live in this house so joyfully. Thank you for allowing me to host and entertain friends, colleagues, have a home office and for all the joy I have found living here. God, I know you must a have a better plan for my life. I know you will make clear to me. I do want to ask for a few things and if they are in alignment with your plan, I'd really love to stay in the same neighborhood, same block would be great, I wouldn't mind being closer to the beach And I wouldn't mind sharing with someone for a year. I am open to the truth you will reveal to me. AMEN"

Two days after I put in "my order", my old roommate called and said he had to move as well. We decided to look together. Four days later, four houses closer to the beach on my street, there was a FOR RENT sign. I called immediately and was informed that there were 11 applications ahead of us. I asked to submit one anyway. We sent it in with the reasons that it should be ours and let it go. I was excited to move in and thought about how it was going to feel to live there as I wrote the letter and filled out the application. I didn't let doubt enter my mind even with so many applications ahead of ours. We were Approved!! I lived in that house for almost 7 years. When you ask clearly for what you want, the universe conspires to bring it to you. Sometimes it shows up how you asked and sometimes it looks completely different than you imagined but fulfill you so much more.

Let's Go Lakers

When we get to the chapter on "The Ritual", we will talk about creating in an affirmative way. You will have the opportunity to write down your intentions. One year on my list I wrote: " I am attending more live events, especially, Laker Games." Within that year and many to follow, I was spontaneously given tickets by co-workers, vendors, and friends. Out of the blue, my neighbors asked if I was interested in working with them at Lakers Games. I was able to be on the court before and after the games. I got to sit in Phil Jackson's chair once (Zen Master) and I even got to wear a championship ring. And since I refer to The It has been a fun manifestation and I had no idea the many ways it would show up.

Concert Tickets

Along with the "Live Event" manifestation, I was asking for Concert tickets. I have been given, invited to and moved at concerts in so many beautiful ways.

One year a friend and I got tickets for Stevie Wonder and Friends at the Hollywood Bowl. I saw that Dolly Parton was playing the next night and the tickets were very inexpensive. The night of the Stevie Wonder concert my friend asked if I'd want to do a "3 Night Stand" at the Bowl. She was given tickets to Train and Maroon 5. I was up for it, as I love live music. Each night we moved closer to the stage. On the last night I said, "Too bad that we aren't coming tomorrow because it would be nice to sit in the boxes." Just as Train finished their set my friend received a text from her girlfriend asking if we'd like to move into the box seats!! AWESOME! And YES!!!

I am a HUGE Beatles Fan and I saw that Paul McCartney was playing at Dodgers Stadium. Paul McCartney hadn't been back since the Beatles played there in 1963. I decided not to buy tickets because I was trying to keep within my budget for the month. A week before the show I was hearing other people were getting excited to go to the show and I declared "I want to go!" The show was sold out for months. The ticket services had nosebleeds seats for $400+/ticket. I still thought, "I am to go see Paul McCartney with affordable tickets!!!" The next day, I was included in a group text from a co-worker saying that he purchased better seats for he and his wife and he had 2 tickets in the upper terrace at face value. I snatched them up immediately. I was beyond excited. I called my concert buddy and we were good to go. The morning of the Paul McCartney concert, I got an email listing upcoming concerts; Justin Timberlake was on the list. Man, I wanted to go to that concert too and also passed on tickets when they first went on sale. I declared in that moment, "I am going to the JT concert." I said to the Universe: "Thank you for showing me the manifestation of the Paul McCartney tickets. I want you know how much I appreciate all the wonderful things you bless me with. If it isn't too much to ask I would really love Justin Timberlake tickets too! Thank you. Thank you. Thank you." I had no idea how and I trusted that the universe was working it out. I headed out to pick up my friend and as we were grabbing dinner before the show. When we sat down to eat she said she had a gift for me. She got better seats for Justin Timberlake for her Daughter's Birthday and she wanted to gift me the original tickets that she bought. HECK YES! I found out I was going to Justin Timberlake on the way to Paul McCartney! LIFE IS MORE THAN GOOD! So in this very happy energy we get to Dodger's stadium and we dance in to The Beatles "Money". On the way to find our seats, were approached by a man who said, "Hello Ladies, it looks like you are here to have a great time." I replied: "We sure are." He said: "If you promise not to scream, how would you like to sit in the 1st row?"

I reached out and HUGGED him and said: "I didn't scream!" My friend realized what was happening and screamed a little. We got down to our seats and we were not only 1st row, we were 1st row center. I was standing 15 ft. from Sir Paul McCartney! Even better than I could have imagined. This stuff works. My manifestations are always trying to find me and sometimes the way they do blows my mind.

The Ritual – Calling in the New

To prepare for the Ritual you will need the following:
A Journal
A Candle
Sage/Palo Santo/Lavender or Smudging Spray
An Open Mind
Small slips of blank paper
A Brown Bag or Box
Champagne, Sparkling Wine or Apple Juice
At least one friend to ground your intentions
& raise the vibration

The class I teach is called, "Calling in the New." In order to invite our hearts desire into our lives we need to clear out all that didn't work, what doesn't work for us. Sometime these things are easy to identify and sometimes they are hidden. We may not realize that we have kept ourselves stuck by our thinking or fear of change. Now is the perfect time to clear the way and be ready to receive the wonderful life you dream of.

The Ritual – Meditation

Before you start it is important to ground yourself and prepare for this clearing. If you meditate regularly then you know how important this is. If you are new to mediation, it's easy with practice. We must shake off anything that has happened before this moment. Stand up and shake your arms and body. Be as silly as possible.

Here is a quick meditation that I use often: Sit with your feet flat on the ground. Take 3 long deep breaths. Visualize that you are a big beautiful tree. Root yourself to the earth. Visualize roots coming out from the bottom of your feet growing deeper and deeper into the earth. As you reach the center of the earth you feel the warm magma on your roots. Feel it moving up the roots, over your feet, up your ankles, calves, thighs, genitals, booty, hips, over your stomach, up your torso, up your back, spine, up your chest, up to your collarbone, over your shoulders, down your arms, down into your fingers tips. Now feel it going back up your arms, to your shoulders, up your neck over your chin, lips, nose, eyes, up your forehead, over the crown, down the back of your head, and as you see it coming back up to the crown of your head visualize that red liquid bursting into the sky and connecting with bright, warm, white light of the heavens. As you take your next breath imagine that white light moving back into your body, following the same path to the center of the earth. It flows through your leaves, branches, trunk, roots nourishing and strengthening you. As the light spreads through you it presses any negative energy out through ends of your roots. And it dissolves from this space you can begin.

You can find other meditations on YouTube, Vimeo or a Google Search

The Ritual – Releasing

This is the time to dig deep. Be honest and perhaps ask friend to help. Really look at what habits, behavior, people have not helped in your growth. These could be laziness, procrastination, smoking, or being a workaholic. Our minds are full of false beliefs. We may have created negative beliefs about ourselves. This time, right now, is for releasing these beliefs. Releasing all that no longer serves us. Releasing guilt, lack, limitation, conditioning from our families, feelings of unworthiness, depression, unhealthy relationships, resentment, anger any and all of these things, people, jobs, etc. Think of the previous year, month, week and what didn't work. Expand to your life leading up to this point. Write down on small slips of paper what you'd like to forget. Drop them in a bag or box. Release, release, release what didn't work, what doesn't work.

I love this quote for the experience or a person: Whether you pushed me or pulled me, drained me or fueled me, loved me or left me, hurt me or helped me, you were a part of my growth and I want to say thank you!

The Next Step is to wrap the bag/box in black paper sealing in the sorrow and hard luck. Saying "good riddance".
Toss the box in the fireplace/outside trash and burn/throw away the past.
Chill some bubbly & honor the old year with a farewell toast.
Remember that every single experience is for our growth. Thank the experience, person and release. As you Toast say, "Thank you and I release you."

The Ritual – Setting Intentions

A new story in life is waiting to be created, embraced and loved. Answers to be discovered and then lived in this transformative ritual of delight and self-discovery instead of wishes or hopes. Write down your hearts desires. Those longings you have kept hidden away until the time seemed right – trust that now is the time. Believe the GIVER OF DREAMS is just waiting to be asked to help you make your dreams come true.
This can't be limited by anything but our own beliefs and conditionings. Dream big. There is a loving source just waiting to answer. I believe that if we are not hurting ourselves or anyone else there is no reason that we should not receive all we desire.

Write your intentions in an affirmative way. Non-affirmative example: "I'm out of debt". Affirmative example: " I am financially free"
Leave out: I am trying, I would like to and I will. Stick to phrases such as: I have a new home, I am living joyfully with my divine right partner, I am continuing to enjoy fulfilling work, etc.

Write down your wishes. Little and BIG! When we write down our wishes with clarity the universe delivers. We need to believe it! If you say it and don't believe it's possible, you'll attract what you truly believe. What is standing in your way of believing you can have it? What can you do to change that belief?

Questions to answer:
What would you like to have happen in your life? What would you like to do, to accomplish? How will you grow spiritually? What do you want to learn?
What good would you like to attract in your life? What areas of growth would you like to have happen to you? What blocks or character defects would you like to have removed?
What would you like to attain? Little things? Big things? Where would you like to go? What would you like to have happen in friendships and love? What would you like to have happen in your family life? How will you grow closer to your partner?

It is important to remember that we can't control other people with our intentions.

We are asking for what our hearts and lives are calling for with the intentions. We ask for our highest good and the highest good of everyone involved. We can't make a Boss get fired, or someone fall in love with you, or your little Brother stop being a brat!

What problems would you like to see solved? How much would you like to have in your savings account? What decisions would you like to make? What would you like to happen in your career? What would you like to see happen inside and around you?

Write it down. Affirm it and let it go.

Like a chapter in a book, your new life is waiting to be written.

Be realistic:

We should Dream Big and also ask for achievable goals. Example: As I mentioned, I always want my team to win, but I remember it's a game where there can only be one winner. Don't be disappointed if these goals don't manifest into you teams perfect season. Also, don't be so attached to the way you think it will show up you miss when it actually does. Just because you have a crush on a certain person doesn't mean you have not attracted love. Be open and ask for healthy reciprocal love to come in. If you write down the qualities of the relationship such as, kind, smart, attractive to me, sexy, self-supporting in all ways, respectful, romantic, great communicator and not "Brown Hair", "Green Eyes", etc. You will more than likely get your perfect match.

If you are making $30k per year and ask for $1,000,000 per year, it may be harder for you to believe in the possibility. It doesn't mean that it is impossible. Just remember that we need to hold our beliefs, so do yourself a favor and don't set yourself up for failure. Let the universe work the rest out.

Be Bold:

Let your mind wrap around the possibility that the things you want most are already allocated to you by the infinite universe.

The Ritual - Giving Thanks

When we are grateful for what we have, we receive more good in our lives. Be in an attitude of gratitude and express your appreciation often. We must be thankful where we are. Right here. Right now. Be grateful for the people in your life, for their friendship, love and to God, the Universe and/or Source. There is nothing more perfect than this moment. We all have these intentions, goals and dreams and we cannot fully be in the moment if we are always negating how good life is right NOW!

The Ritual - Feeling Into It

In addition to writing down our intentions we need to feel into them. What I mean by this is, if you are wishing for your divine right partner, then imagine what it feels like when you are together. Perhaps you get a cute text, a gentle kiss, or a warm hug. What joy you feel as you laugh, travel and cook together. If your intention is for a wonderful job with great people then imagine how it feels in your body when you sign the contract, you are in your new office and interacting with your co-workers.

The Ritual - Declaration

Now that you have set your intentions you should read them out loud with your intention setting partner or the intention setting group. During this reading you will be releasing these wishes to the Universe for their fulfillment.

The Ritual – Letting it go

We make our wishes and then we let them go. We must not limit the universe. We have limited minds. The Universal Mind sees so much more than we do. It is our job to ask for dreams in our hearts to manifest. It is not to control how that happens. It may not be the brown haired girl who will own your heart or the blue-eyed boy you envisioned. The partner you ask for may look different from your celebrity crush and yet, he or she will posses all the qualities and attractiveness you'll desire.

Manifesting Vision Boards

I am sure you have heard about vision boards and how with picture and words you can draw into your life what you desire. There are many different ways to Create Vision Boards. You can divide into categories Travel, Love, Money, and Career. On the next page is an example board. The only "RIGHT" way is the one that works for you.

What you will need…

Construction Paper
Glue
Magazines to cut images and words
An hour or two to dedicate

There are a few things that are important to remember when creating your board. Make sure the words you are using build you up and do not break you down. For example: "I am Healthy" instead of just "Weight Loss". It is important to feel into each word and picture to make sure it resonates within you before placing it on your board.

If you are looking for more fulfillment in your current career or looking for a new job you may find pictures of office buildings or work stations you like. Make sure that you cover up logos if you don't want to work only at that company. You can use words like "Accomplished", "Wonderful Work", "Financial and Personal Wealth". Make sure you feel into how each image and word makes you feel. If there is any anxiety then choose another image.

Calling in your partner, if you are using pictures as a general "type" you are attracting then make sure you cover their eyes with words like "Love", "Joy", "Communication" or any word that represents the qualities you'd like your partner to have.

If I use a picture of Johnny Depp, I want to make sure I am not sitting around waiting for Johnny to knock on my door and ignoring any other potential partners who may present themselves. You can use images of what your ideal Girl or Guy looks like and modify as noted above.

<u>Sample Vision Board</u>

Above is an example of a board in progress. Images cut and arranged before gluing. Each Section can have its own piece of construction paper that you can tape together when designing your board. You can use colored paper or crayons if you want to add color. You can also hand write words if you can't find them and paste them on your board. This is a guideline. You'll notice that words and pictures represent what we are calling in to our lives. This board includes Career, Love, Life, Health, Travel and the World. If you want a new car, a new home, new job, new love, yours will look different. The good news is that you have free reign. It's your vision, your board, so you can create anything your heart desires.

<u>Finished Vision Board</u>

The Rialto Bridge

On one of my vision boards I included a photo of Venice, Italy. I have wanted to visit since I was teenager. The photo was taken on the Rialto Bridge. When I joyfully found myself in Venice, Italy in 2011, I was taking tons of photographs. When I got back home and was looking through my photos, one looked beyond familiar. I looked on my Vision Board and I had taken a shot that matched almost perfectly the photo on my vision board. This Stuff Works!

Manifestation Flower

I was thinking of an easy way to describe the process of manifestation for a class I was facilitating called "Spring Forward".
I came up with a "Manifestation Flower". This flower has four parts that are essential to their beautiful appearance.

1. The Earth / Soil
2. The Roots / Stem
3. The Leaves
4. The Petals

Using the 4 parts we are going to identify your goals and create a visual reference to guide you and direct your energy.

Construction Paper
A print out of the Manifestation Flower
Glue
Magazines to cut images and words
A few hours

Take a piece of construction paper and start building a visual of your goals/dreams/future

The Earth/Soil – What seeds have you planted to move you towards your goals? How have you tended to the soil? Are there any weeds need to be pulled? (Write those down and discard before starting.)

The Roots/Stem – What brings you back to center? What reminds you to refocus? Is it going to the beach? Working out? Meditation? A Walk? Yoga?

Leaves – What supports you and keeps you on track? Uplifting music, dancing, church, spiritual practice, laughter, meditation, and/or yoga?

The Petals of the flowers are what you are blossoming into...

A Loving Relationship
A New Career
Better Health
Healing
Financial Abundance
A New Home
Travel
New Car
New Exercise Routine
New Wardrobe

Sample Board using two Manifestation Flowers

Manifestation Flower

Manifestation Flower to copy

Homework

Gratitude lists: Take your journal or use notes on your "smart phone" every morning and write @ least one thing you are grateful for. Repeat before you go to bed. Do it everyday for one year. Even if it is: " I opened my eyes". "I'm grateful that I am breathing".

Clearing any time "throughout the year":
The clearing fire/trash ritual can be practiced through out the year. You can look up the new moon calendar and create a monthly ritual of calling in/releasing during that time as well. You may hear that the Full Moon is great for releasing and the New Moon is great for creating. This is true but anytime you feel the need, is the perfect time.

God boxes: You can write down what troubles you and/or what you'd like help resolving and put them in a small box. These are often called "God Boxes" as you are giving your troubles to God. When we hand our troubles over we no longer need to concern ourselves with them. Just trust that they will be handled. Empty this out every month and see how problems so large in the moment have faded away.

Meditation: So much pressure is put on silent meditation and how to do it right. I was the girl who thought, "I can't meditate", so when I discovered guided meditation I was in heaven. I have found that once I started be consistent with guided meditations incorporating a few minutes of silence got easier and easier. If thought come in just allow them to float through and focus on your breath. While in the shower image it's a tropical waterfall. The water is falling over you and washing troubles down the drain.

Daily positive quotes:
There are many calendars & books available to inspire everyday of the year! Start your day with some inspiration!!

Tarot/angel/word for the day cards:
I love these!! They are a nice way to center in on a feeling tone for the day. I'll ask what do I need to know today? And I generally pick the perfect card for what is happening in my life at the time.

Clearing Energy / Cord Cutting:
All day, everyday we interact with others. Sometimes this is positive and sometimes it's not. It is important to clear your energy. "Thank you for all the interactions I had today, I clear myself of all energy that does not belong to me or is not of love." A good book on Cord Cutting is "Cutting the Cord" by Marcella Kroll.

Spiritual practice / studies:
Create your own. I believe we are all sparks of GOD. Created from the same source no matter what anyone chooses to call it. Shape your practice the way that makes your heart happy. At the heart of all faiths I believe is the Golden Rule. I start from there. And make kindness my religion.

Affirmations:
It is a good idea to keep our thoughts up and positive. Affirmations are great for shifting any negative self-talk we may have. You can grab some Post It's and place affirmations on your bathroom mirror or around your house.

If you are a guy who is a perfectionist you could say something like "I am a successful, accomplished, productive man. I am at peace in this moment with what is." If you are a woman who beats herself up over weight, feel you are able to trust in relationships or you have low self esteem. You could say something like, "I am a Confident, Healthy, Trustworthy Woman/Man and I thrive in my relationships."

What Students Have to Say…

Dawn is an exceptional teacher. Her end of the year Manifestation class was eye opening, fun, and very centering. I felt clear, inspired, and in control of my life when I left the class that evening. She had us follow up with a partner from class to confirm goals and desires and that really helped solidify what I wanted to bring into my life. Dawn is wise and intuitive. She practices what she preaches and brings a great deal of knowledge and experience to her classes. – Julie Corson

Dawn is truly an inspiration! I attended her class, "Calling in the New Year" during a time in my life when I needed some emotional support and guidance. Dawn helped me release what wasn't working in my life and gave me the direction I needed to set my goals both personally and professionally. Dawn has a very powerful intuition and natural gift for helping people! I would highly recommend her book to anyone who is on a path of self-development and growth. – Gina Costello

Dawn is a major manifestor with proven results.
Her skills at manifesting WORK!
Using the tools I learned in the workshop, I have manifested wonderful things in my life!
– Wendy Allamby

I participated in Dawn's "Calling in the New" manifesting class in 2014. It was an eye opener and I continue to use the tools I learned in my daily life. Dawn is a fantastic teacher and I definitely recommend her process. – Lisa Loehrlein

Special Thanks

Dr. Maisha Hazzard

Dr. Alexina Hazzard

Dr. Annette Eggleston

Ellen Butler

Michelle Bronson

Jeff Segal &
Mystic Journey Bookstore

Lauren Simpson

Leslie Conliffe

Johnny Brown

Everyone who has participated in my workshops

All the Angels who have blessed my life!

References

"Simple Abundance a Daybook
of Comfort and Joy"
Sarah Ban Breathnach

"The Language of Letting Go"
Melody Beattie

"The Secret"
Rhonda Byrne

" The Law of Attraction"
Ester and Jerry Hicks

"A Wish Can Change Your Life"
Simon & Shuster

Khepra Institute of Applied Metaphysics
and the Center for Inner Peace
http://khepra-institute.org/

About the Author...

Manifesting is the magic of having what you dare to imagine show up in your life. Dawn Hoffman, a native of New York who grew up in Southern California, is a gifted Manifestor who has chosen to share the miracle of intention, focus and practice within this book.

Dawn has been manifesting throughout her life by refusing to accept limitations. She learned to be fearless which helped her to move beyond what appeared to be her destiny. Challenging situations became magical experiences.

Dawn believes we are manifesting all of the time whether we realize it or not. As a freelance commercial producer she has been able to do many things that keep her busy. dawnhofmancreative.com

Here is the short list:

- Non profit organization founder of " A Walk in My Shoes" focusing on junior high school students by bringing speakers who tell their story of overcoming and succeeding http://www.awalkinmyshoesinc.com/
- Art Show Curator
- Fundraiser and Event Producer
- Photography and Photo Card Sales
- Spiritual Counselor
- Intuitive Coach
- Ordained Minister
- Documentary Producer - "Seeking God"
- #The Human Race Project - exploration into unity of all people as one race without need to separate (on YouTube: #thehumanrace)
- Seminar Leader and Workshop Facilitator
- Created the "God's Time Clock" available on www.cafepress.com
- Author of "Words My Soul Spoke Through My Hand", "The White Horse Repair Kit for When Prince Charming Seems Broken", and "9 Stories"
- Co-Creator of Appreciation Memo by Impossible Colors.

This book has been created by Dawn to share the understanding, processes and techniques that have been used successfully by her clients to manifest experiences, material things, relationships, travel, projects and finances. After teaching for more than 6 years at Mystic Journey Book Store in Venice, California it became clear that what she had been offering would be good for a larger audience.
Her hope is that the reader will discover the magic of manifesting.

Manifestations

Made in the USA
Middletown, DE
17 August 2022

71563635R00029